I0886259

Slippers!

INTRODUCTION

Someone always needs a new pair of slippers! Nine styles are included in this leaflet, six to crochet and three to knit.

Instructions for each style are written, using Worsted Weight yarn, in six sizes for women and children.

These slippers make perfect gifts for friends and family, and are great items for bazaars and fairs.

We hope that you enjoy the selection and that you find the instructions easy to follow. Please let us know if you have any questions or comments.

Table of Contents

1. Pom-Pom Slippers to crochet.......... 3
2. Moccasins to crochet.......... 4
3. Foot Warmers to crochet.......... 5
4. Tied Instep to crochet.......... 8
5. Ballet Slippers to crochet.......... 9
6. "Pixies" to crochet.......... 10
7. After Ski Boots to knit.......... 12
8. Ruffle Top to knit.......... 14
9. Garter Stitch to knit.......... 15

General Instructions.......... 16

Leisure Arts • Maumelle Arkansas

1
6
5
2

1. POM-POM SLIPPERS to Crochet

(Shown on page 2)

by Frances Baltich; Stockton, CA

	Children's			Women's		
Size:	Small	Medium	Large	Small	Medium	Large
Sole Length:	7½"	8"	8½"	9"	9½"	10"

Size Note: Instructions are written for Children's sizes in first parentheses with Women's sizes in second parentheses. Instructions will be easier to read, if you circle all the numbers pertaining to your size.

MATERIALS

Worsted Weight Yarn, approximately:
(2-2½-3)(3-3½-3½) ounces,
[(60-70-90)(90-100-100) grams]
Crochet hook, size G (4.5 mm)
or size needed for gauge
Yarn needle

GAUGE: 16 sc and 16 rows = 4"

TOP

Instep

Beginning at Toe, ch (5-5-7)(7-9-9) **loosely**.

Row 1: Sc in second ch from hook and in each ch across; ch 1, turn: (4-4-6)(6-8-8) sc.

Row 2 (Increase row)**:** 2 Sc in first sc, sc in each sc across to last sc, 2 sc in last sc; ch 1, turn: (6-6-8)(8-10-10) sc.

Rows 3 and 4: Sc in each sc across; ch 1, turn.

Row 5: Repeat Row 2: (8-8-10)(10-12-12) sc.

Rows 6-9: Sc in each sc across; ch 1, turn.

Row 10: Repeat Row 2: (10-10-12)(12-14-14) sc.

Repeat Row 9, (1-2-3)(4-5-6) times.

At end of last row, ch (33-35-37)(39-41-43) **loosely** for Heel.

Side

Remove hook from ch, insert hook in first sc of last row and, being careful **not** to twist ch, insert hook into last loop on ch and pull through.

Begin working in rounds.

Rnd 1: Ch 1, sc in next ch and in each ch across, sc in edge of each (11-12-13)(14-15-16) rows along side of Instep; working in free loops of beginning ch, 2 sc in first ch, sc in next (2-2-4)(4-6-6) chs, 2 sc in last ch; sc in edge of each (11-12-13)(14-15-16) rows along second side of Instep: (60-64-70)(74-80-84) sc.

Note: Do not join at end of rounds. Using a 2" scrap piece of yarn, place marker at beginning of rounds, moving marker after each round is completed.

Rnds 2 and 3: Sc in each sc around.

Rnd 4: Sc in next (14-15-16)(17-18-19) sc, 2 sc in next sc, sc in next 2 sc, 2 sc in next sc, sc in next (26-28-31)(33-36-38) sc, 2 sc in next sc, sc in next 2 sc, 2 sc in next sc, sc in each remaining sc: (64-68-74)(78-84-88) sc.

Rnds 5 and 6: Sc in each sc around; at end of Rnd 6, slip st in next sc, finish off.

SOLE

Beginning at Toe, ch (5-5-7)(7-9-9) **loosely**.

Row 1: Sc in second ch from hook and in each ch across; ch 1, turn: (4-4-6)(6-8-8) sc.

Row 2 (Increase row)**:** 2 Sc in first sc, sc in each sc to last sc, 2 sc in last sc; ch 1, turn: (6-6-8)(8-10-10) sc.

Row 3: Sc in each sc across; ch 1, turn.

Rows 4-6: Repeat Rows 2 and 3, once; then repeat Row 2 once **more**: (10-10-12)(12-14-14) sc.

Repeat Row 3, (19-21-23)(25-27-29) times.

Decrease Row: Decrease (***see Decreasing, page 16***), sc in each sc to last 2 sc, decrease; ch 1, turn: (8-8-10)(10-12-12) sc.

Next 2 Rows: Sc in each sc across; ch 1, turn.

Repeat Decrease Row, 2 times: (4-4-6)(6-8-8) sc.

At end of last row, do **not** ch 1; finish off.

FINISHING

Join pieces as follows: Place Top on Sole with **wrong** sides together. Join yarn with slip st at Heel; working through **both** pieces, slip st in each sc of Top easing in Sole fullness; join with slip st to first st, finish off.

Edging: With **right** side facing, sc around entire opening, decreasing 4 sts at Heel, and one st at each corner of Instep; join with slip st to first sc, finish off.

Add pom-pom ***(Figs. 6a-c, page 16)***.

2. MOCCASINS to Crochet

(Shown on page 11)

by Modene Thornton; Little Rock, AR

	Children's			Women's		
Size:	Small	Medium	Large	Small	Medium	Large
Sole Length:	7½"	8"	8½"	9"	9½"	10"

Size Note: Instructions are written for Children's sizes in first parentheses with Women's sizes in second parentheses. Instructions will be easier to read, if you circle all the numbers pertaining to your size.

MATERIALS

Worsted Weight Yarn, approximately:
(2-2½-3)(3½-3½-4) ounces,
[(60-70-90)(100-100-110) grams**]**
Crochet hook, size G (4.5 mm)
or size needed for gauge
Yarn needle

GAUGE: 16 sc and 16 rows = 4"

SOLE & SIDE

Sole

Ch (23-25-25)(27-27-29) **loosely**.

Rnd 1: 2 Sc in second ch from hook, sc in next (8-9-9)(10-10-11) chs, hdc in next 3 chs, dc in next (7-8-8)(9-9-10) chs, 2 dc in next ch, hdc in next ch, 5 sc in last ch; working in free loops of beginning ch ***(Fig. 5, page 16)***, hdc in next ch, 2 dc in next ch, dc in next (7-8-8)(9-9-10) chs, hdc in next 3 chs, sc in next (8-9-9)(10-10-11) chs, 2 sc in last ch: (51-55-55)(59-59-63) sts.

Note: Do **not** join at end of rounds, unless otherwise specified. Using a 2" scrap piece of yarn, place marker at beginning of rounds, moving marker after each round is completed.

Rnd 2: 2 Sc in each of next 2 sts, sc in next (21-23-23)(25-25-27) sts, (2 sc in next st, sc in next st) twice, 2 sc in next st, sc in next (21-23-23)(25-25-27) sts, 2 sc in each of last 2 sts: (58-62-62)(66-66-70) sc.

Rnd 3: Sc in next sc, 2 sc in next sc, sc in next (22-24-24)(26-26-28) sc, (2 sc in next sc, sc in next 2 sc) 3 times, 2 sc in next sc, sc in next (22-24-24)(26-26-28) sc, 2 sc in next sc, sc in last sc: (64-68-68)(72-72-76) sc.

Rnd 4: Sc in next sc, 2 sc in next sc, sc in next (25-27-27)(29-29-31) sc, (2 sc in next sc, sc in next 2 sc) 3 times, 2 sc in next sc, sc in next (25-27-27)(29-29-31) sc, 2 sc in next sc, sc in last sc: (70-74-74)(78-78-82) sc.

Children's size Large ONLY and ALL Women's sizes - Rnd 5: Sc in next sc, 2 sc in next sc, sc in next (30)(32-32-34) sc, (2 sc in next sc, sc in next 2 sc) 3 times, 2 sc in next sc, sc in next (30)(32-32-34) sc, 2 sc in next sc, sc in last sc: (80)(84-84-88) sc.

Women's sizes Medium and Large ONLY - Rnd 6: Sc in next sc, 2 sc in next sc, sc in next (35-37) sc, (2 sc in next sc, sc in next 2 sc) 3 times, 2 sc in next sc, sc in next (35-37) sc, 2 sc in next sc, sc in last sc: (90-94) sc.

Side - ALL SIZES

Rnd 1: Remove marker, slip st in next st, ch 2 **(counts as first hdc)**, hdc in same st, skip next sc, ★ 2 hdc in next sc **(Shell made)**, skip next sc; repeat from ★ around; join with slip st to top of beginning ch-2 **(now and throughout)**: (35-37-40)(42-45-47) Shells.

Rnd 2: Ch 2, **turn**; hdc in same sp, Shell in sp between each Shell around; join.

Repeat Rnd 2, (2-2-2)(3-3-3) times.

Next Rnd: Ch 2, **turn**; hdc in same sp, Shell in next (8-9-9)(10-11-11) sps, ch (7-7-9)(9-11-11) **loosely** for Strap, skip next (17-17-20)(20-21-23) sps, work Shell in last (9-10-10)(11-12-12) sps; join: (18-20-20)(22-24-24) Shells.

Next Rnd: Ch 2, **turn**; hdc in same sp, Shell in each sp across to ch, Shell in first ch, ★ skip next ch, Shell in next ch; repeat from ★ across chs, Shell in each remaining sp; join: (21-23-24)(26-29-29) Shells.

Repeat Rnd 2, (1-1-1) (2-2-2) time(s).

Next Rnd: Ch 1, do **not** turn; sc in each hdc around, decreasing 4 sts at Heel ***(see Decreasing, page 16)***; join to first sc.

Reverse Single Crochet Edging (Right side)**:** Ch 1, do **not** turn; working from **left** to **right**, ★ insert hook in sc to **right** of hook ***(Fig. 1a)***, hook yarn and draw through, under and to left of loop on hook (2 loops on hook) ***(Fig. 1b)***, YO and draw yarn through both loops on hook ***(Fig. 1c)* (reverse single crochet made, *Fig 1d*)**; repeat from ★ around; join to first st, finish off.

Fig. 1a

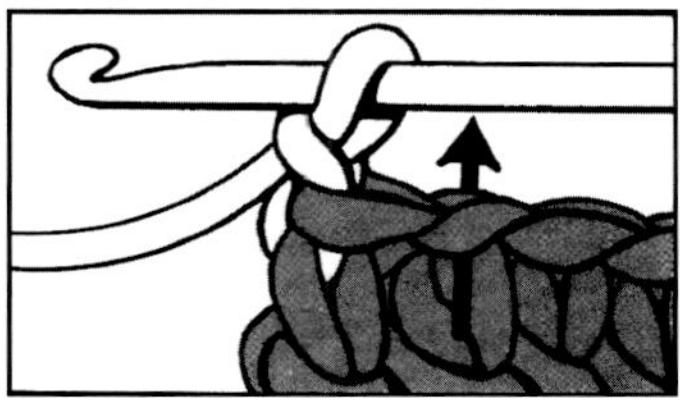

Fig. 1b

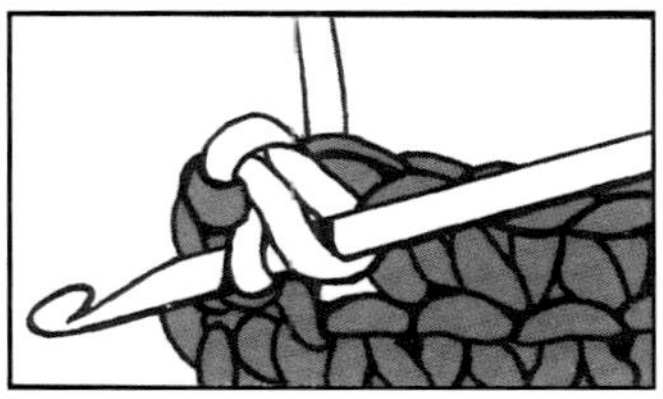

Fig. 1c

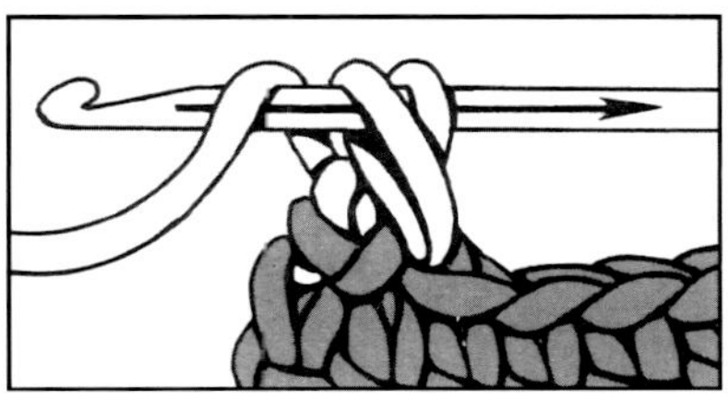

Fig. 1d

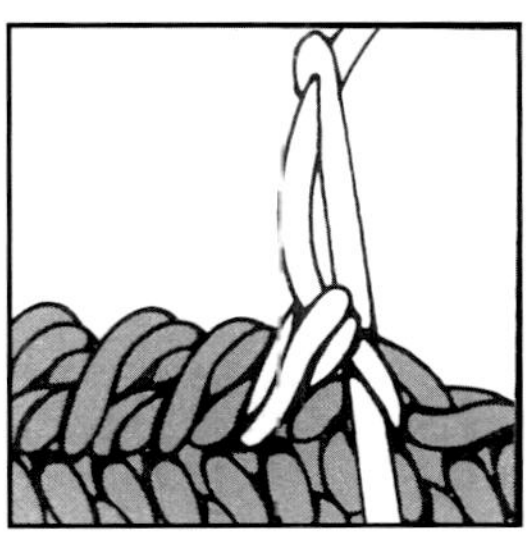

INSTEP

Ch (23-25-25)(27-27-29) **loosely**.

Rnd 1: 2 sc in second ch from hook, sc in each ch to last 3 chs, 2 sc in next ch, sc in next ch, 5 sc in last ch; working in free loops of beginning ch, sc in next ch, 2 sc in next ch, sc in each ch to last ch, 2 sc in last ch; do **not** join, place marker: (51-55-55)(59-59-63) sc.

Complete same as Sole, beginning with Rnd 2.

At end of last round; slip st in next st, finish off.

FINISHING

Join pieces as follows: Place toe of Instep on unfinished edge of Side with **wrong** sides together. Join yarn with slip st at Strap; working through **both** pieces, slip st evenly around; finish off.

3. FOOT WARMERS to Crochet

(Shown on page 7)

by Frances Baltich; Stockton, CA

	Children's			Women's		
Size:	Small	Medium	Large	Small	Medium	Large
Sole Length:	7½"	8"	8½"	9"	9½"	10"

Size Note: Instructions are written for Children's sizes in first parentheses with Women's sizes in second parentheses. Instructions will be easier to read, if you circle all the numbers pertaining to your size.

MATERIALS

Worsted Weight Yarn, approximately:
- Main Color - (1½-2-2½)(2½-3-3) ounces, **[**(40-60-70)(70-90-90) grams**]**
- Contrasting Color - (1½-1½-2)(2-2½-2½) ounces, **[**(40-40-60)(60-70-70) grams**]**

Crochet hook, size G (4.5 mm) **or** size needed for gauge

Yarn needle

GAUGE: 16 sc and 16 rows = 4"

Instructions begin on page 6.

TOP

With Main Color ch (40-40-44)(44-48-48) **loosely**; being careful **not** to twist ch, join with slip st to form a ring.

Rnd 1: Sc in each ch around: (40-40-44)(44-48-48) sc.

Note: Do **not** join at end of rounds. Using a 2" scrap piece of yarn, place marker at beginning of rounds, moving marker after each round is completed.

Rnd 2: Sc in each sc around.

Repeat Rnd 2, (5-6-7)(8-9-10) times.

Decrease Rnd: ★ Decrease ***(see Decreasing, page 16)***, sc in next (8-8-9)(9-10-10) sc; repeat from ★ around: (36-36-40)(40-44-44) sc.

Next 3 Rnds: Sc in each sc around.

Decrease Rnd: ★ Decrease, sc in next (7-7-8)(8-9-9) sc; repeat from ★ around: (32-32-36)(36-40-40) sc.

Next 3 Rnds: Sc in each sc around.

Sc in next (18-18-21)(21-24-24) sc, remove marker; ch 1, **turn**.

Instep

Row 1: Sc in first (4-4-6)(6-8-8) sc; ch 1, **turn**.

Repeat Row 1, (13-15-17)(19-21-23) times; at end of last row, do **not** ch 1.

Side

Rnd 1: Place marker, **turn** and work sc in edge of each row along left side of Instep, sc in next 12 sc, 2 sc in next sc, sc in next (2-2-4)(4-6-6) sc, 2 sc in next sc, sc in next 12 sc, sc in edge of each row along right side of Instep, 2 sc in next sc, sc in next (2-2-4)(4-6-6) sc, 2 sc in last sc: (64-68-76)(80-88-92) sc.

Rnd 2: Sc in next (26-28-30)(32-34-36) sc, 2 sc in next sc, sc in next (4-4-6)(6-8-8) sc, 2 sc in next sc, sc in next (26-28-30)(32-34-36) sc, 2 sc in next sc, sc in each sc to last sc, 2 sc in last sc: (68-72-80)(84-92-96) sc.

Rnd 3: Sc in each sc around.

Rnd 4: Sc in each sc around to last sc, sc in next sc to last step, cut Main Color, with Contrasting Color complete last sc.

Rnds 5-7: Sc in each sc around.

Slip st in next sc; finish off.

SOLE

Beginning at Toe with Contrasting Color, ch (5-5-7)(7-9-9) **loosely**.

Row 1: Sc in second ch from hook and in each ch across; ch 1, turn: (4-4-6)(6-8-8) sc.

Row 2 (Increase row)**:** 2 Sc in first sc, sc in each sc to last sc, 2 sc in last sc; ch 1, turn: (6-6-8)(8-10-10) sc.

Row 3: Sc in each sc across; ch 1, turn.

Rows 4-6: Repeat Rows 2 and 3, once; then repeat Row 2 once **more**: (10-10-12)(12-14-14) sc.

Repeat Row 3, (19-21-23)(25-27-29) times.

Decrease Row: Decrease, sc in each sc to last 2 sc, decrease; ch 1, turn: (8-8-10)(10-12-12) sc.

Next 2 Rows: Sc in each sc across; ch 1, turn.

Repeat Decrease Row, 2 times: (4-4-6)(6-8-8) sc.

At end of last row, do **not** ch 1; finish off.

FINISHING

Join pieces as follows: Place Top on Sole with **wrong** sides together. Join Contrasting Color at Heel; working through **both** pieces, sc in each sc of Top **and** in each sc or row of Sole; join with slip st to first sc, finish off.

Cuff: With **wrong** side facing, join Contrasting Color with slip st to top edge at back.

Rnd 1: Ch 1, sc in same st and in each sc around; join to first sc.

Rnd 2: Ch 1, sc in same st and in each sc around; join to first sc, finish off.

Trim: With two strands of Contrasting Color and using Photo as a guide, outline Instep with back stitch.

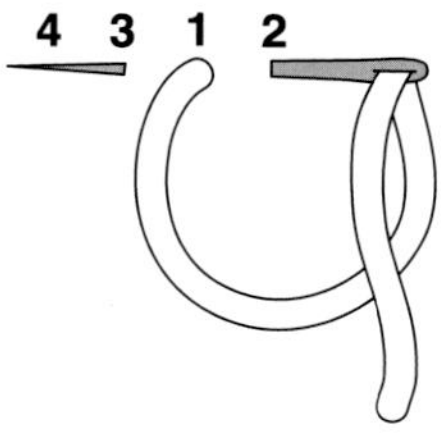

3
4

4. TIED INSTEP to Crochet

(Shown on page 7)

by Dorothy Miller; Canton, OH

	Children's			Women's		
Size:	Small	Medium	Large	Small	Medium	Large
Sole Length:	7½"	8"	8½"	9"	9½"	10"

Size Note: Instructions are written for Children's sizes in first parentheses with Women's sizes in second parentheses. Instructions will be easier to read, if you circle all the numbers pertaining to your size.

MATERIALS

Worsted Weight Yarn, approximately:
(3½-4-4½)(4½-5-5) ounces,
[(100-110-130) (130-140-140) grams**]**
Crochet hook, size I (5.5 mm)
or size needed for gauge
Yarn needle

GAUGE: With one strand of yarn, 14 sc = 4"
With two strands of yarn held together,
13 sc = 4"

SIDE (Make 2)

Starting at bottom edge with **one** strand of yarn, ch (27-29-31)(33-34-36) **loosely**.

Row 1: Sc in second ch from hook and in each ch across; ch 1, turn: (26-28-30)(32-33-35) sc.

Row 2 (Decrease row)**:** Decrease **2 times** for Toe ***(see Decreasing, page 16)***, sc in each sc across; ch 1, turn: (24-26-28)(30-31-33) sc.

Row 3 (Decrease row)**:** Sc in each sc to last 2 sc, decrease **once** for Toe; ch 1, turn: (23-25-27)(29-30-32) sc.

Repeat Rows 2 and 3, (3-3-3)(3-4-4) times; then repeat Row 2, (0-0-1)(1-0-1) time(s): (14-16-16)(18-18-18) sc.

At end of last row, ch 1, sc in edge of each row across; finish off: (9-9-10)(10-11-12) sc.

Join yarn with slip st at opposite end; ch 1, sc in edge of each row across; finish off: (9-9-10)(10-11-12) sc.

SOLE

With **two** strands of yarn held together, ch (6-6-8)(8-9-9) **loosely**.

Row 1: Sc in second ch from hook and in each ch across; ch 1, turn: (5-5-7)(7-8-8) sc.

Row 2: Sc in each sc across; ch 1, turn.

Repeat Row 2 for a total of (44-46-50)(52-55-59) rows; at end of last row, do **not** ch 1 or turn, finish off.

FINISHING

Right Side

Sole Foundation Row: Join **one** strand of yarn with slip st in last st worked; ch 1, sc in edge of each row; ch 1, turn: (44-46-50)(52-55-59) sc.

Joining Row: Place Heel edge of Right Side on top of Sole, ch 1; working through **both** pieces, sc in first (8-8-9)(9-10-11) sc, 2 sc in next sc; working across bottom edge, sc in next (26-28-30)(32-33-35) sc, working across Toe edge, 2 sc in next sc, sc in remaining sc; finish off.

Left Side

Sole Foundation Row: Join **one** strand of yarn with slip st in edge of first row on side (Heel edge) not yet joined; ch 1, sc in edge of each row; ch 1, turn: (44-46-50)(52-55-59) sc.

Joining Row: Place Toe edge of Left Side on top of Sole, ch 1; working through **both** pieces, sc in first (8-8-9)(9-10-11) sc, 2 sc in next sc; working across bottom edge, sc in next (26-28-30)(32-33-35) sc; working across Heel edge, 2 sc in next sc, sc in remaining sc; do **not** finish off.

Edging

Ch 1, working across Left Side, decrease, sc in next (5-6-6)(7-7-7) sc, make a 1½" chain, sc in remaining sc across Side, sc in first (2-2-3)(3-4-4) sc across Front, make a 1½" chain, sc in each sc across Side to last 2 sc, decrease, decrease (2-2-2)(2-3-3) sts evenly across Heel; join with slip st to first sc, finish off.

Tie

With **two** strands of yarn held together, chain a (19-19-20)(20-21-21)" length; finish off.

Lace through side loop, front loop, and last loop.

Add pom-poms ***(Figs. 6a-c, page 12)*** to each end of chain.

5. BALLET SLIPPERS to Crochet

(Shown on page 2)

by Modene Thornton; Little Rock, AR

	Children's			Women's		
Size:	Small	Medium	Large	Small	Medium	Large
Sole Length:	7½"	8"	8½"	9"	9½"	10"

Size Note: Instructions are written for Children's sizes in first parentheses with Women's sizes in second parentheses. Instructions will be easier to read, if you circle all the numbers pertaining to your size.

MATERIALS

Worsted Weight Yarn, approximately:
(2-2½-3)(3-3½-3½) ounces,
[(60-70-90)(90-100-100) grams]
Crochet hook, size G (4.5 mm)
or size needed for gauge
Yarn needle

GAUGE: 16 sc and 16 rows = 4"

SOLE

Ch (23-25-25)(27-27-29) **loosely**.

Rnd 1: 2 Sc in second ch from hook, sc in next (8-9-9)(10-10-11) chs, hdc in next 3 chs, dc in next (7-8-8)(9-9-10) chs, 2 dc in next ch, hdc in next ch, 5 sc in last ch; working in free loops of beginning ch ***(Fig. 4, page 12)***, hdc in next ch, 2 dc in next ch, dc in next (7-8-8)(9-9-10) chs, hdc in next 3 chs, sc in next (8-9-9)(10-10-11) chs, 2 sc in last ch: (51-55-55)(59-59-63) sts.

Note: Do **not** join at end of rounds, unless otherwise specified. Using a 2" scrap piece of yarn, place marker at beginning of rounds, moving marker after each round is completed.

Rnd 2: 2 Sc in each of next 2 sts, sc in next (21-23-23)(25-25-27) sts, (2 sc in next st, sc in next st) twice, 2 sc in next st, sc in next (21-23-23)(25-25-27) sts, 2 sc in each of last 2 sts: (58-62-62)(66-66-70) sts.

Rnd 3: Sc in next st, 2 sc in next st, sc in next (22-24-24)(26-26-28) sts, (2 sc in next st, sc in next 2 sts) 3 times, 2 sc in next st, sc in next (22-24-24)(26-26-28) sts, 2 sc in next st, sc in last st: (64-68-68)(72-72-76) sts.

Rnd 4: Sc in next st, 2 sc in next st, sc in next (25-27-27)(29-29-31) sts, (2 sc in next st, sc in next 2 sts) 3 times, 2 sc in next st, sc in next (25-27-27)(29-29-31) sts, 2 sc in next st, sc in last st: (70-74-74)(78-78-82) sts.

Children's size Large ONLY and ALL Women's sizes - Rnd 5: Sc in next st, 2 sc in next st, sc in next (30)(32-32-34) sts, (2 sc in next st, sc in next 2 sts) 3 times, 2 sc in next st, sc in next (30)(32-32-34) sts, 2 sc in next st, sc in last st: (80)(84-84-88) sts.

Women's sizes Medium and Large ONLY - Rnd 6: Sc in next st, 2 sc in next st, sc in next (35-37) sts, (2 sc in next st, sc in next 2 sts) 3 times, 2 sc in next st, sc in next (35-37) sts, 2 sc in next st, sc in last st: (90-94) sts.

TOP - All Sizes

Rnd 1 (Wrong side)**:** Slip st in next st, ch 2 **(counts as first hdc)**, **turn**; hdc in next st and in each st around, remove marker; join with slip st to top of beginning ch-2: (70-74-80)(84-90-94) hdc.

Note: Work Bubble as follows: **[**YO, insert hook around st just made ***(Fig. 2a)***, YO and bring hook back**]** 3 times, YO and draw through all loops ***(Fig. 2b)***.

Fig. 2a

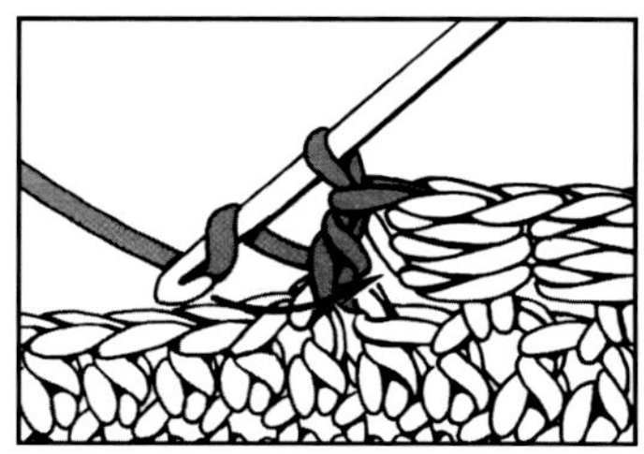

Fig. 2b

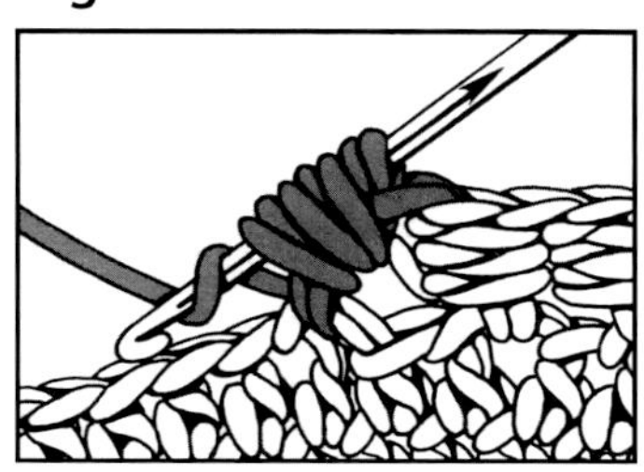

Rnd 2: Ch 2, **turn**; work Bubble, skip next st, ★ hdc in next st, work Bubble, skip next st; repeat from ★ around; join with slip st to top of beginning ch-2: (35-37-40)(42-45-47) Bubbles.

Rnd 3: Ch 1, **turn**; sc in first (29-31-34)(36-39-41) sts, (skip next st, sc in next st) 6 times, sc in remaining sts; join with slip st to first sc: (64-68-74)(78-84-88) sts.

Rnd 4: Ch 2, turn; work Bubble, skip next st, ★ hdc in next st, work Bubble, skip next st; repeat from ★ around; join with slip st to top of beginning ch-2: (32-34-37)(39-42-44) Bubbles.

Rnd 5: Ch 1, **turn**; sc in first (27-29-32)(34-37-39) sts, (skip next st, sc in next st) 5 times, sc in remaining sts; join with slip st to first sc: (59-63-69)(73-79-83) sts.

Rnd 6: Ch 2, **turn**; work Bubble, (skip next st, hdc in next st, work Bubble), (9-10-12)(13-14-15) times, skip next 2 sts, dc in next st, work Bubble, (skip next 2 sts, tr in next st, work Bubble) 4 times, skip next 2 sts, dc in next st, work Bubble, skip next 2 sts, (hdc in next st, work Bubble, skip next st), (10-11-12)(13-15 -16) times; join with slip st to first st: (26-28-31)(33-36-38) Bubbles.

Rnd 7 (Decrease rnd)**:** Ch 1, **turn**; decrease twice (***see Decreasing, page 12***), sc in next (16-18-21)(23-26-28) sts, decrease 6 times, sc in each st to last 4 sts, decrease twice; join to first st: (42-46-52)(56-62-66) sts.

Rnd 8 (Right side): **Turn**; slip st in each sc around; join to first st, finish off.

6. "PIXIES" to Crochet

(Shown on page 2)

by Ruth Shepherd; Chickasaw, AL

	Children's			Women's		
Size:	Small	Medium	Large	Small	Medium	Large
Sole Length:	7½"	8"	8½"	9"	9½"	10"

Size Note: Instructions are written for Children's sizes in first parentheses with Women's sizes in second parentheses. Instructions will be easier to read, if you circle all the numbers pertaining to your size.

MATERIALS

Worsted Weight Yarn, approximately:
(2-2½-3)(3-3½-3½) ounces,
[(60-70-90)(90-100-100) grams**]**
Crochet hook, size E (3.5 mm)
or size needed for gauge
Yarn needle

GAUGE: 18 hdc and 12 rows = 4"

HEEL

Ch (16-16-18)(19-21-23) **loosely**.

Row 1: Hdc in third ch from hook and in each ch across; working in free loops of beginning ch, hdc in each ch across and in turning ch; ch 2 **(counts as first hdc)**, turn: (30-30-34)(36-40-44) hdc.

Row 2: Hdc in next hdc and in each hdc across; ch 2, turn.

Repeat Row 2 for a total of (10-10-11)(11-12-12) rows.

At end of last row, ch (22-22-24)(24-26-26) for Instep; being careful not to twist ch, join with slip st to first hdc of last row, finish off.

TOE

Begin working in rounds.

Rnd 1: Skip first (14-14-16)(17-19-21) hdc from edge (where ch was joined), join yarn with slip st in next hdc, ch 2, turn; hdc in each hdc and ch around; join with slip st to first hdc **(now and throughout)**: (52-52-58)(60-66-70) hdc.

Rnd 2 (Decrease rnd)**:** Ch 2, turn; hdc in next (25-25-28)(29-32-34) hdc, place marker using a 2" scrap piece of yarn, skip next 2 hdc, hdc in remaining hdc; join with slip st to first hdc: (50-50-56)(58-64-68) hdc.

Rnd 3 (Decrease rnd)**:** Ch 2, turn; hdc in next hdc and in each hdc to within one st of marker, move marker, skip next 2 hdc, hdc in remaining hdc; join with slip st to first hdc: (48-48-54)(56-62-66) hdc.

Repeat Rnd 3, (11-12-13)(14-15-16) times: (26-24-28)(28-32-34) hdc.

Remove marker.

Next Rnd: Ch 1, turn; decrease over next 2 sts (***see Decreasing, page 12***) (13-12-14)(14-16-17) times; join with slip st to first st, finish off leaving a 10" end: (13-12-14)(14-16-17) sts.

Thread needle with end and weave through remaining sts, pulling to close Toe; finish off.

CUFF

With **right** side facing, join yarn with slip st in edge of last row worked.

Row 1: Ch 2, working in edges of rows, hdc evenly across Heel; hdc in edge of each row; ch 2, turn.

Row 2: Hdc in each hdc across; ch 2, turn.

Repeat Row 2, (1-1-1) (3-3-3) time(s).

Finishing Rnd: Sc in each hdc across, ch 1, sc in edge of each row along side of Cuff, ch 1; working in free loops of each ch across Instep, sc in first(10-10-11)(11-12-12) chs, 3 sc in each of next 2 chs, sc in remaining chs, ch 1, sc in edge of each row along side of Cuff; join to top of turning ch, finish off.

2

8

7. AFTER SKI BOOTS to Knit

(Shown on page 13)

by Bev Dillon; Bellevue, WA

	Children's			Women's		
Size:	Small	Medium	Large	Small	Medium	Large
Sole Length:	7½"	8"	8½"	9"	9½"	10"

Size Note: Instructions are written for Children's sizes in first parentheses with Women's sizes in second parentheses. Instructions will be easier to read, if you circle all the numbers pertaining to your size.

MATERIALS

Worsted Weight Yarn, approximately:
- Main Color - (3-3½-4)(4-4½-4½) ounces, **[**(90-100-110)(110-130-130) grams**]**
- Contrasting Color - (1-1-1)(1½-1½-1½) ounce(s), **[**(30-30-30)(40-40-40) grams**]**

Knitting needles, size 7 (4.5 mm) **or** size needed for gauge
Crochet hook (for Tie)
Yarn needle

GAUGE: With two strands of yarn held together, in Garter Stitch **or** in Stockinette Stitch, 16 sts = 4"

SOLE

With two strands of Main Color held together, cast on (60-64-68)(72-76-80) sts **loosely**.

Note: In Garter Stitch (knit every row), two rows form one ridge.

Work in Garter Stitch until there are (7-7-8)(8-9-9) ridges.

SIDES

Cut **one** strand of Main Color and add **one** strand of Contrasting Color.

Row 1 (Eyelet row)**:** K2, YO, K2 tog, knit across to last 4 sts, K2 tog, YO, K2.

Row 2 (Decrease row)**:** K4, P2 tog, purl across to last 6 sts, P2 tog through the back loop, K4: (58-62-66)(70-74-78) sts.

Row 3 (Decrease row)**:** K4, slip 1 as to **knit**, K1, pass the slipped st over, knit across to last 6 sts, K2 tog, K4: (56-60-64)(68-72-76) sts.

Row 4 (Decrease row)**:** K4, P2 tog, purl across to last 6 sts, P2 tog through the back loop, K4: (54-58-62)(66-70-74) sts.

Row 5 (Decrease **and** Eyelet Row)**:** K2, YO, K2 tog, slip 1 as to **knit**, K1, pass the slipped st over, knit across to last 6 sts, K2 tog twice, YO, K2: (52-56-60)(64-68-72) sts.

Repeat Rows 2-5, (1-2-3)(1-2-3) time(s): (44-40-36)(56-52-48) sts.

Repeat Rows 2-4 once: (38-34-30)(50-46-42) sts.

Repeat Rows 1-4, (2-1-0)(3-2-1) time(s): (26-28-30)(32-34-36) sts.

CUFF

Cut Contrasting Color and add second strand of Main Color.

Row 1 (Eyelet row)**:** K2, YO, K2 tog, knit across to last 4 sts, K2 tog, YO, K2.

Rows 2-4: Knit across.

Rows 5-8: Repeat Rows 1-4.

Bind off all sts.

FINISHING

Fold piece in half; sew bottom and toe seam.

Tie: With **two** strands of Main Color held together, chain a (37-37-37)(37-40-40)" length; finish off.

Lace through Eyelets as for a shoe and tie in a bow at the ankle.

9
7

8. RUFFLE TOP to Knit

(Shown on page 11)

by Ruth Shepherd; Chickasaw, AL

	Children's			Women's		
Size:	Small	Medium	Large	Small	Medium	Large
Sole Length:	7½"	8"	8½"	9"	9½"	10"

Size Note: Instructions are written for Children's sizes in first parentheses with Women's sizes in second parentheses. Instructions will be easier to read, if you circle all the numbers pertaining to your size.

MATERIALS

Worsted Weight Yarn, approximately:
(2-2½-3)(3-3½-3½) ounces,
[(60-70-90)(90-100-100) grams**]**
Knitting needles, size 9 (5.5 mm)
or size needed for gauge
Yarn needle

GAUGE: In Garter Stitch (knit every row),
16 sts and 32 rows = 4"

Beginning at Heel,
cast on (26-26-30)(32-36-38) sts **loosely**.

Work in Garter Stitch until piece measures (5¾-5¾-6¾)(6¾-7¾-7¾)".

Decrease Row: K2 tog, knit across to last 2 sts, K2 tog: (24-24-28)(30-34-36) sts.

Continue to decrease one st at **each** side, every other row, 4 times **more**: (16-16-20)(22-26-28) sts.

Cut yarn leaving a long end, thread needle with end and draw through remaining sts, pulling to close Toe.

Sew center front seam to within (3¾-3½-3¾)(4-4¾-4½)" of cast on edge or to desired opening.

RUFFLE CUFF

With **right** side facing, pick up one stitch in edge of each row along opening ***(Fig. 3)***.

Row 1: Increase in each st across (knit in front and in back of each st).

Rows 2-6: Work in Garter Stitch.

Bind off all sts.

Sew back seam.

PICKING UP STITCHES

Insert needle under two strands at the edge of the worked piece. Put the yarn around the needle and pull it through, making a stitch on the needle.
Repeat along the edge, picking up the required number of stitches ***(Fig. 3)***.
A crochet hook may be helpful to pull yarn through.

Fig. 3

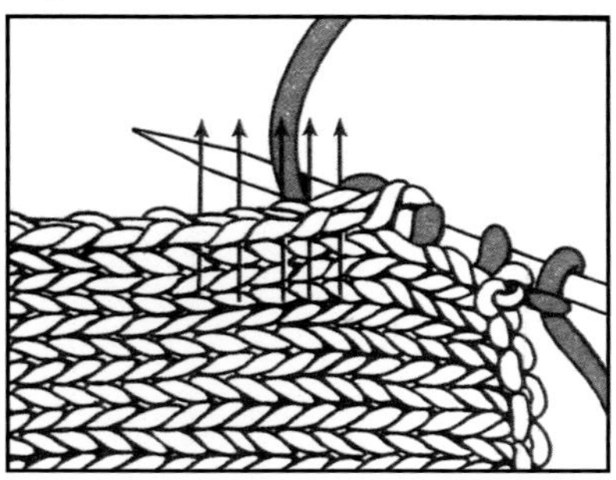

9. GARTER STITCH to Knit

(Shown on page 13)

by Bev Dillon; Bellevue, WA

	Children's			Women's		
Size:	Small	Medium	Large	Small	Medium	Large
Sole Length:	7½"	8"	8½"	9"	9½"	10"

Size Note: Instructions are written for Children's sizes in first parentheses with Women's sizes in second parentheses. Instructions will be easier to read, if you circle all the numbers pertaining to your size.

MATERIALS

Worsted Weight Yarn, approximately:
(2-2½-3)(3-3½-3½) ounces,
[(60-70-90)(90-100-100) grams]
Knitting needles, size 9 (5.5 mm)
or size needed for gauge
Crochet hook (for Tie)
Yarn needle

GAUGE: In Garter Stitch (knit every row),
16 sts and 32 rows = 4"

HEEL

Cast on (38-38-42)(44-48-50) sts **loosely**.

Row 1: K (13-13-14)(15-16-17), P1 (turning ridge), K (10-10-12)(12-14-14), P1 (turning ridge), knit across remaining sts.

Row 2 (Eyelet row)**:** K3, K2 tog, YO, knit across to last 5 sts, YO, K2 tog, K3.

Row 3: K (13-13-14)(15-16-17), P1 (turning ridge), K (10-10-12)(12-14-14), P1 (turning ridge), knit across remaining sts.

Row 4: Knit across.

Repeat Rows 1-4 until there are (8-8-9)(9-10-10) Eyelet rows, ending by working Row 3.

TOE

Row 1: Bind off 5 sts, knit across: (33-33-37)(39-43-45) sts.

Row 2: Bind off 5 sts, K (7-7-8)(9-10-11), P1, K (10-10-12)(12-14-14), P1, knit remaining sts: (28-28-32)(34-38-40) sts.

Row 3: Knit across.

Row 4: K (8-8-9)(10-11-12), P1, K (10-10-12)(12-14-14), P1, knit remaining sts.

Repeat Rows 3 and 4 until piece measures (7-7½-8)(8½-9-9½)" from cast on edge.

Decrease Row: K2 tog across: (14-14-16)(17-19-20) sts.

Next Row: Knit across.

Repeat Decrease Row once.

Do **not** bind off.

FINISHING

Cut yarn leaving a long end, thread needle with end and draw through remaining sts, pulling to close Toe.

Sew center front seam.

Beginning at top edge, sew back seam to turning ridge, weave through remaining sts, pulling to close Heel.

Tie: Chain desired length; finish off.

Lace through Eyelet row and tie in front.

GENERAL INSTRUCTIONS

ABBREVIATIONS

ch(s)	chain(s)	Rnd(s)	Round(s)
dc	double crochet	sc	single crochet(s)
hdc	half double crochet(s)	sp(s)	space(s)
K	knit	st(s)	stitch(es)
mm	millimeters	tog	together
P	purl	tr	treble crochet(s)
		YO	yarn over

SYMBOLS & TERMS

★ – work instructions following ★ as many **more** times as indicated in addition to the first time.

( ) or **[ ]** – work enclosed instructions **as many** times as specified by the number immediately following **or** contains explanatory remarks.

GAUGE

Correct gauge is essential for proper fit of Slippers. Needle or hook sizes given in instructions are merely guides and should never be used without first making a sample swatch approximately 4" square in the stitch, yarn, and needle or hook specified. Then measure it, counting your stitches and rows carefully. If you have more stitches per inch than specified, try again with a larger size needle or hook; if fewer, try again with a smaller size. Keep trying until you find the size that will give you the specified gauge. **DO NOT HESITATE TO CHANGE NEEDLE OR HOOK SIZE TO OBTAIN CORRECT GAUGE.**

DECREASING in Crochet

Decreases are made by working the established stitch to within one step of completion, working the next stitch to the same point, then completing the last step of both stitches at the same time ***(Fig. 4)***, making one stitch over two of the previous row.

Fig. 4

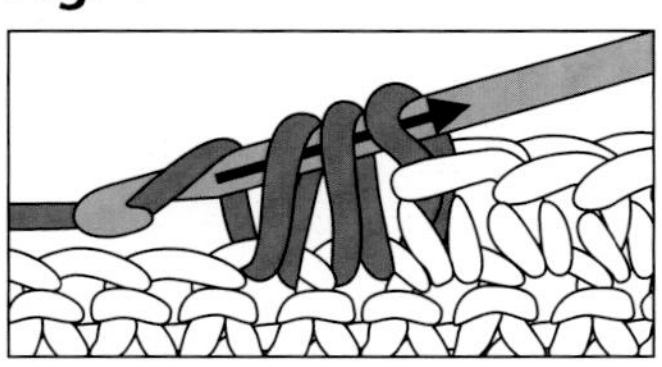

FREE LOOPS OF A CHAIN

When instructed to work in free loops of a chain, work in loop indicated by arrow ***(Fig. 5)***.

Fig. 5

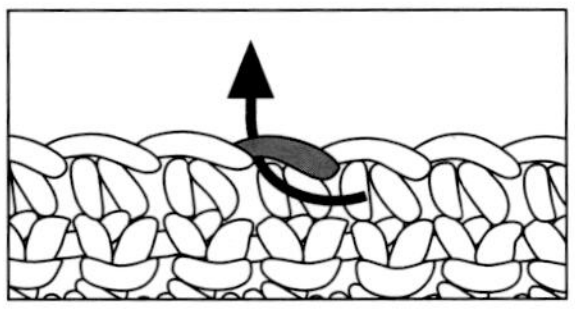

POM-POM

Cut a piece of cardboard 3" wide and as long as you want the diameter of your finished pom-pom to be. Wind the yarn around the cardboard until it is approximately ½" thick in the middle ***(Fig. 6a)***. Carefully slip the yarn off the cardboard and firmly tie an 18" length of yarn around the middle ***(Fig. 6b)***. Leave yarn ends long enough to attach the pom-pom. Cut the loops on both ends and trim the pom-pom into a smooth ball ***(Fig. 6c)***.

Fig. 6a

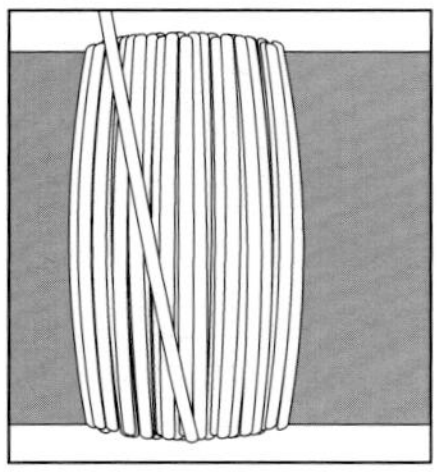

Fig. 6b

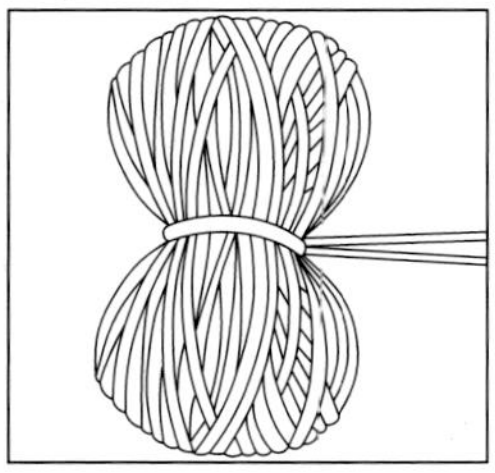

Fig. 6c

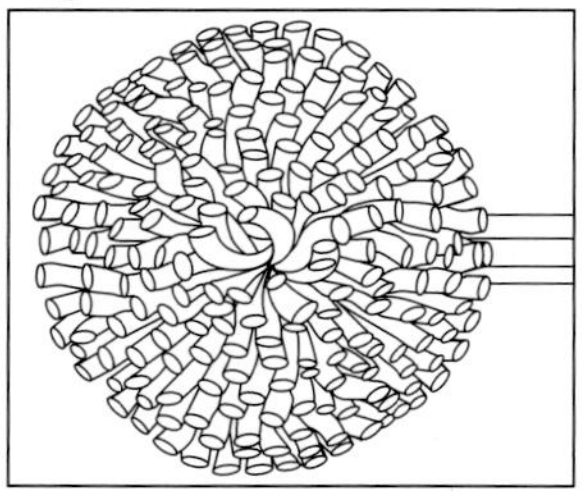

FINISHING

Make a habit of taking care of loose ends as you work. To keep loose ends from showing, always weave them back through several stitches or work over them. When ends are secure, clip them off close to work.

Slippers made and instructions tested by Jo Ann Bowling, Margaret Bredlow, Fran Carman, Marie Creston, Lois Davis, Ruth Forster, Linda Graves, Maria Harris, Gerri Johnson, Geraldine Johnston, Marge Lyp, Diane Menzies and Kathleen Wilson.

Made in U.S.A.